The Ultimate
Budget Planner

Money Management and
Personal Finance Tips to
Get Rid of Debt Fast!

Table of Contents

Introduction

All of us have some debts that are in our lives. We went to college and need to pay off some debts, we have a car loan to deal with, or we have a few too many credit cards to pay off. We have been taught that debt is a part of life, something that we have to deal with, and this can make it really difficult to get ahead, to start saving, getting a retirement started, or doing some of the other great things that we want in life.

This guidebook has some of the solutions that you need in order to finally get your money in line. All of us are able to budget for the things in life that we need and it is possible to pay off those debts, but it is time to get serious about the work and actually work hard to make it a reality. This guidebook will provide you with some of the tools that you need to take those debts and make them go away.

Inside this guidebook, we are going to spend a lot of time talking about how to create a budget and how to get our debts in line. We will start with some basics about why being debt free is such a great idea and how you can be intentional with your work. We can then work on creating a budget and figuring out where you are now compared to where you would like to be in the future. Knowing where your money is right now and where it is going can help you to get things in order.

We then move on to some other important topics that you need in order to get things in line. This guidebook will talk about some of the steps that you can take to accelerate your debt payoffs, how to control some of your expenses and income, how to avoid common money traps, and even how to invest your money to help you get ahead. Your retirement account, your savings account, reducing your taxes, and some ways to cut down on your bills are also discussed in this guidebook to help you get a full picture of your finances and how you can make them better.

In this guidebook, we strive to help you get a full picture of your finances and where you are able to make some changes. If you are able to follow some of the tips in this guidebook and make them work for your needs, you are sure to see some great changes in the amount of debts that you owe and the amount of financial freedom that you will be able to enjoy!

Anyone is able to reach financial freedom, they just need to take a stand against their debts and become intentional in their efforts to finally get some of the debts all paid off. It is going to be hard work and it is going to take some time, but with some deliberate hard work and organizing your finances, it is something that you can get done in no time!

When you are ready to finally cut down some of that debt and you want to reach financial freedom, make sure to check out this guidebook today to help you get started!

Chapter 1: Understanding the Reasons to be Debt Free

Most of us have to deal with some kind of debt. We are told that this is normal, that it is the only way that we are able to get the things that we want out of life. We may have credit card debt, student loan debt, debt on our homes, and so much more. If you are able to live without any debt, you are ahead of most people in this country.

The issue is that while we are told that debt is a good thing, it is really bad for us. It let's us feel comfortable spending money that we don't have. It can cost us thousands of dollars each year to pay the interest off, and it can even make it hard to get a home or other investments later on because we have some debt.

Now there are different kinds of debts. Some people see student loans as a good debt because it is an investment into their future careers and as long as you pay it off right away and you don't take out more than necessary, it may not be bad. Purchasing a home may give you a lot of debt overall, but it is often seen as an investment and since you are able to sell the home if needed, it usually isn't counted in this bad debt.

The debt that we are talking about in this guidebook includes things like credit card debt, loans for vacations, loans for home improvements, and even auto loans. These are not investments, rather they are more money that is wasted in interest rates over time. These debts can keep you away from a future that you are looking for and can keep you from reaching your goals.

Some debts, like what you owe for housing each month, whether it is through rent or your mortgage, are not going to count because there isn't too much you can do about them. You could move into a place that charges less rent or purchase a home that has a lower mortgage, but you would still need to pay these bills.

The first thing that you need to do is understand that you don't need to be in debt in order to make it through life. It is not like there are laws in place or like there is someone who is able to force you into debt if you don't feel like it. You are able to go to school and not accumulate debt (or at least go to one that is cheaper and easier to pay off). You can wait to purchase a home or save up to earn a vacation or a new car rather than using a loan for it.

Of course, if you have already gone to school and received this debt, you have to deal with it, but it doesn't mean that you have to stay in debt for the remainder of your life.

Once you are able to get rid of the debt that you are dealing with, you will find that getting out of debt can be so liberating and it is going to make you feel really good. Despite the idea that our society has about debt just being a part of life, there are actually millions of people who will see that you are debt free and they will feel jealous about the fact that you are able to remain debt free.

Despite the fact that there are a lot of people who are in debt, it is possible to break out of the whole system and become debt free, no matter how much debt you have taken on. While it is going to take a bit of time to get started with being debt free, there are a number of benefits for this.

One of the first benefits is that you can gain a lot of freedom from being debt free. This is often one of the biggest motivators that can occur when you are trying to pay everything off. They are going to pay off the bills that they have, while thinking about how great they will feel when they get all of their bills paid off. They will own the things they have rather than dealing with payments forever.

You will be able to own the objects that you want, rather than paying a ton of interest for years to someone else to have the product. You won't have to worry as much about losing your job or a bad economy because you just have the minimum payments to make each month rather than paying back all of those loans.

When you are able to pay off the debts that you owe, you can take that extra money to put into savings, into a retirement, or to use in other ways that you like, rather than always having to worry about paying of that money to a big bank all of the time.

In addition to being able to feel some of that freedom that you crave so much, you will also be able to affect some of the others who are around you. With the money that you save from not having to pay these bills any longer, you will be able to do a lot of cool things with your life.

You may be able to take your parents out to enjoy a great meal every once in a while rather than worrying about putting food on the table each night.

You can send your child to a nicer school if you would like, give to a charity in your area, or just place it into a savings account to save for retirement or other things that you would like. You will be able to do so much good in the world if you don't have to focus so much on the money that you have to pay back to someone else through your debts.

These are just a few of the reasons why you may want to work on becoming debt free. Each person is going to have their own personal reasons for wanting to be debt free and as long as it motivates you to be successful at paying off the debt, it doesn't really matter what the reasons are.

Now that we know some of the benefits that come with being debt free, let's take a look at some of the ways that you are able to actually get rid of your debt and live a life where you control your money each month!

Chapter 2: Deciding to be Intentional

So the goal of this book is to help you to become debt free. If you would like this to happen, you need to learn how to be intentional. You will never be able to see a good reduction in the amount of debt that you have if you refuse to start a budget or you keep spending your money on things that are frivolous and aren't needed. If you aren't able to keep some of these at bay, you are going to have trouble with paying off the debts that you want.

This means that one of the first things that you will need to do in order to get that debt paid off is to set up a budget. When you have a budget in place, you will be able to see how much money is coming in and how much you are able to spend each month.

This budget is going to help you to see better where you can make some cuts in your spending and how you can place that money towards paying off the debts faster compared to what you do now.

The first thing that we are going to look at is how to create our own budgets. To start, you need to find all of your bank statements for the last six months or so and your bills for at least the last couple of months so that you can find some averages to work with. Bring in some pen and paper to help you to find out the numbers that you need.

Look at your bank statement and see how much money you are bringing in from your job, your spouses job, and anywhere else. Write this number down at the top on the page.

After we know how much money we should have to work with each month, it is time to look at how much we are spending and even what we are spending that money on.

First, we are going to write down the bills that are required to pay each month. This would include things like our housing expenses, food, and any of the debts that you have to pay each month. Write this number down and see where you are from here.

After those numbers are ready, it is time to go through and see what other things you are paying for. This would include expenses aren't necessary, such as that daily run to the coffee shop, cable, internet, nights going out and so on.

These can really bite into your income and if you are able to cut some of them out slowly, you will find that your income is going to clear up quite a bit and it may be easier to get some of those debts paid off.

Once you have all of those numbers written down, you should have a better idea of where all of your money is going. Does this number come up even with your current income, does it leave you will a little bit extra that you are able to put towards paying down the debts or into savings, or are you falling behind with your current spending?

Regardless of the answer that you are getting here, you may still see some places where you are able to cut the spending a little bit and these changes will allow you to cut down on the debts faster than before.

For example, are you still paying $100 for cable and barely watching it? You could cut that out and get Hulu or Netflix for about $10 a month, saving quite a bit of money each month.

Are you still paying for a gym membership that you visit once or twice a month? Those can often cost $70 or more each month and cutting that out and working out at home can save a lot of money.

Getting movies from the local library or switching around with your friends can save on movie night and eating in rather than going out a few times a week can really free up some of the money. In this chapter, we are being intentional, so you need to make sure that you are going through every part of your budget and finding as many things that you are able to cut as possible.

So now that you have an idea of what things you are spending unnecessarily on, it is time to go through and cancel the things that are costing you too much and that you just don't need anymore. You will find that this could save you a lot of money that you could use for paying off some of your debts.

Remember that when you cut out these excess spending areas, you need to be intentional. This means that if you save some money on a gym membership, that money needs to go to paying off your debt, rather than using it to go out more or to purchase more things.

In the beginning, you may only be able to save a few dollars here and there to help out with the debt, but anything is better than nothing and it does add up over time. Over time, you will be able to cut down on the debs that you have. When you get one debt paid down, the trick is to either put that extra money into savings each month or use that extra money to pay off some more of the debts so that you can get them all done with.

There are many methods that you can use that will help you to pay off some of the debts that you are dealing with, but you need to make sure that you are intentional with your plans. Sometimes creating a budget and seeing where all of your finances are will make a big difference in the frame of mind that you will be in.

Most of us are in denial about our debts and we assume there is nothing that we are able to do to eliminate the debts. But with a deliberate plan and a good budget in place, it is easier to see where the cuts need to come from and to eliminate them as much as possible.

Chapter 3: Figuring Where Your Finances Are Right Now

In the previous chapter, we spent some time looking at the benefits of setting up a budget. This is a great way to help you to sort out your finances and determine what money you have coming in, what money you are spending on debts and housing expenses, and what money you are just throwing away on things that are not really needed.

The budget is a really great way to get a good look at your financial situation right now. Without having a good idea of where your finances are right now, it is hard to understand what bills you are paying, how you can make changes, or even how to get more of the debts paid off in a timely manner.

Remember that during this process, getting out of debt is going to take determination and a little bit of time. We all wish that we were able to get rid of the debt overnight without a lot of hassle, but this is just not going to happen. It takes just a few minutes to get more debt, but it takes a long time before you are able to pay it off. Make sure to keep this in mind before getting started so you don't get upset that it takes a bit or that things aren't moving along as quickly as you would like.

Many people want to get those debts paid off in no time, and that is admirable, but it is not realistic. You only have so much income and it will take a bit of time to get those debts paid off with your current income.

When you are creating the budget that you want to use on your family, you are getting the opportunity to go through all of the different aspects that are making up your finances. You know that you bring in a certain amount of income each month and you will be able to learn exactly where all of your debts are coming from each month.

You will even learn where some of the extra expenses are going and it can help you to figure out if you are really making enough money to get through each month.

Some people find that they are already doing a good job and if they cut back just a bit more, they could put some money into their savings or more towards paying off the bills.

Others are going to find that they are already in way over their heads' and they may need to go through and make some changes to see results or to even make it through each month on their current lifestyle.

The budget can be hard for some people to do because it makes you take a good hard look at the different things that you are doing with your money and some people do not want to have to look at this all of the time.

You don't want to be stuck dealing with debt forever or paying a lot of extra money because of some high interest rates, but even though it is hard, a budget is the only way for you to see where your finances are right now so you can make a good plan of where you want to go.

Sometimes the budget is going to tell you that you are doing a great job and can show you some ways that you can make changes to start paying the debts down faster than ever.

Other times it is going to tell you that your finances are a mess and that you may need to completely change your personal spending habits or cut out a lot of extras that you enjoy so that you can just pay off the debts that you want and use that money for other things in your life, like having fun.

 It may seem like a headache when you are first getting started on this journey, but it really does help you to get on the right track to paying off those debts and reaching your financial freedom.

Chapter 4: Mapping Out Your Plan

Now that we have taken some time to create a new budget and figure out where we would like to go with our financial plan, it is time to use that budget and some of the other tools to make a map of where we would like to go. It isn't going to help you out at all if you just sit there and say that you want to pay off debts but you don't put in any of the work to get it done.

There are many questions that you will need to ask yourself in order to get started on this path including: How do I want to pay these debts off?

What things will I need to give up in order to reach this goal? Where is the money going to come from in order to pay off these debts? This is the stage where you will ask a lot of questions and figure out how to get started on paying those debts off.

The first thing that we are going to look at is how we will get those debts paid off. Are you certain that you have the dedication that it is going to take in order to make some extra money or give up some of the things that are needed in order to put more money towards these debts? Will you need to take up a side job in order to make a little bit of extra money?

Of course, that extra job can be hard for some people to pull off, but it can help bring in some extra that could at least be used to pay down those debts and you can always stop once you get a bit ahead. An added bonus is that it takes up some more of your time so you are less likely to spend your money frivolously.

Next, you will also need to take some time to determine how you will pay off some of the debts that you already have. It is important that you make minimum payments on all of the debts that you have.

This helps to protect your credit score and it will help to pay down the debts a little bit, even though this is one of the slowest and most inefficient methods of getting the debts paid off quickly.

If you happen to have a little bit of money left over after paying off your other needs and paying the minimum on your debts, you can take that extra and start paying off some more of your debts, getting that debt paid off faster than before. But never go ahead and skip out on making at least the minimum payments on your debts before moving on.

Before we do anything else, make sure that you have enough money in your budget so that you are able to

pay the minimum on all debts
because this is better than nothing.

Once you are sure that you have this
minimum amount, you will be able to
figure out if there is anything extra
that you can use to put towards one
or two of the debts, something extra
to pay them off a little bit faster in
the long run.

Now there are a few ways that you
can follow in order to pay the debts
that you have and picking one will
depend on the income that you can
put towards them and your overall
objectives.

Most experts will recommend that you take the largest loan, or at least the one with the highest interest rate, and put your money towards that one first. This can be effective because it will help you to save the most money over time.

With this kind of method, it doesn't really matter if you can pay a few dollars extra a month or $300 extra a month, it will all make a big difference in getting that high interest or big loan paid off.

Then the second method is where you are going to choose to pay off some of the smaller amounts of loans first. This one is not going to be the most effective because you are paying more off in interest payments over time, but you are able to pay these smaller loans and debts off faster, which is sometimes a good motivator for some people.

Those bigger debts take a long time to pay off and after some time of not getting rid of them, you can lose some motivation. When you are able to quickly click off those smaller ones, you may gain some more motivation to tackle that big one once you get to it. Plus, you can take the extra money you saved from the smaller loans and make bigger payments on that large one.

Both of these method can be really effective at helping you to cut down your debt and while the first one will often save you the most money over time, either one can be effective based on your budgeting style. You just need to pick one and stick with it for the long term if you want to be able to pay off some of those debts.

No matter which of these methods you are choosing to pay off the debts, you should pick one from the very beginning and then map it out so that you can follow through with it for the whole process. This gives you a good plan and keeps you on track for seeing success and becoming debt free.

Chapter 5: Accelerating the Pace to Pay off Debts Faster

One trick that you need to work on if you would like to get some of these debts paid off is to learn how to accelerate the pace. While it is going to take some time to pay off these debts, you can make the time less if you learn some simple tools to pay off debt quickly.

Most people who get into the idea of being debt free want to be able to get it done as soon as possible and sometimes they will search around in order to find a good method to help them get it done.

It is always a great thing to get excited over paying down debt and that is going to be a good motivator to keep you on the right path. Paying off debt can be exciting, although the work to get it done is usually quite boring so bring that excitement over and get ready to make it all happen as quickly as possible.

At some point, you are probably all ready to get that debt paid down as quickly as possible. You are tired of having them hang around for a long time and you want to be rid of them for good so you want to hurry up the process. The fist thing that you are able to do in order to make this happen is look through the budget.

Yes, you made one at the beginning, but you should have a plan to go through it every six months or so to help you to determine if you are on the right path to seeing your success.

You can cut down on some of the frivolous things that you are spending money on and then use that money to pay down more debts. Sometimes those things that we tried to kick out originally will sneak back n and we need that regular budget check to help out with getting it back in line.

The snowball affect is another great method that you can use to accelerate how fast you are paying off the debts. With this method you are going to tackle one of your debts first. Experts recommend that you start with the debt that is the largest or the one with the highest interest rate.

Any extra money that you are going to throw at the debts you will put towards this one debt, getting it down as much as possible. This may take a few years depending on the debt, but you work to pay this one down as quickly as possible.

Then, when this debt is paid down, it is time to take that money, all the original payment from that debt plus all the extra money, and put it towards a second debt to pay that out. Now that second debt is going to have its minimum payment plus all this extra to help pay it down.

You keep on going with that, adding in the payments from each of the previous debts until all of them are gone. The first debt that you use is going to take a bit, but by the time that you get to the last one, it may have three, four, or even more payments going to it and you can pay it down quickly.

For this one to work, you need to still make the minimum payments on all of your debts, but you will put all of the extra toward the one debt. This helps you to avoid extra interest payments and fees from not paying your obligations. It is a great way to pay down your debts quickly without having to find extra money in your budget each month.

Another thing that you might want to consider in order to accelerate the pace that you are paying off your debts is to get a second job. This would be one that you could fit in at nights or on the weekend when you have some free time and would not conflict with your regular job.

You are not going to be able to pay off your bills if you lose your first job in favor of a part time job or the economy gets bad enough that you can't find a job at all.

You could also consider doing freelance work with something that you enjoy such as tutoring, freelance writing, web page design, and so much more. There are a lot of sites that will allow you to do this work on a schedule that works the best for your needs.

You can then take the money that you are earning and put it straight towards the debt to get it paid off much faster. You could even keep the job after you are done paying the debt off in order to build up some savings to use for other situations.

You will be able to find the second job that works the best for you based on your skills and what you have time for. For some people, this means going to another physical job, and others are able to work from home to make some extra money. But bringing in that extra income can really make all of the difference.

In some cases, you might be able to get some discounts if you make payments on time or if you do things such as direct deposits. These are usually found with things like student loans but it never hurts to ask around about your debt and see if you could get some sort of discount. This is going to allow you to save some money and pay off the debt much faster.

The snowball effect is one of the best options that you can use when it is time to pay off some of your debts. It is highly effective because it makes sure that you are paying the minimum on your debts while also helping you to make other additional payments as well. The first debt is often going to take some time to go away, but as you pay off more and more debts, the process becomes faster, and you are going to finally be debt free!

Chapter 6: Control Your Income and Expenses

Before you are able to manage your money, you need to have a good plan in place in order to control the spending that you do. It does not matter how much money you are bringing in each year if you just turn around and spend all of it before it even gets into your account.

Controlling your income and your expenses can be hard. Here are some of the ways that you can monitor and control your spending so that your money can last much longer.

Budget

Many people who are looking to manage their money will find that it is disappearing and they do not know where it is going. How can you manage money if you do not know where you spend it or where it is coming from?

The first thing that you need to do in order to manage your money is create a budget. This allows you to see what extra things you are spending on and where you can cut back. This simple step can save you a ton of money without having to do a lot of extra work.

Creating a budget can be pretty easy, and we discussed it a bit before in this guidebook, but it is so important to helping you to set up yourself for financial freedom. It gives you a clear picture of the income that you have, what bills you need to pay, and it even makes it easier for you to find places to cut out unnecessary expenses to save you money.

In some cases, this budget is not going to give you the nice picture that you are hoping for. You may see that you are spending way too much money and that you need to make some cuts right away or you are heading to financial ruins.

On the other hand, there are times when your budget may be in a pretty good place and you are already able to throw a bit of money at your debts to help pay them off faster. But no matter which of these categories you fit in, or even if you fit in somewhere in between, there are always things that you are able to cut out of your spending to help pay off those debts.

If you are looking at your budget and notice that it is not giving you some nice numbers, it is time to make some changes. This can be anything from cutting out some of the expenses to cutting up your credit card and even getting a second job. You will have to look at your own unique situation and determine what will work the best to get you to financial freedom.

Monitor Expenses

For a few weeks, you should record all of the things that you are purchasing. Make sure to put down each tank of gas, the drink, soda, piece of clothing, and anything else that you spend your money on. You can then put this information into an Excel spreadsheet and see where the money is going.

You might be surprised at how much you are spending on designer clothes or on that special coffee you like and with a little tweaking, you can end up saving a lot of money with alternative routes while still enjoying both of these things.

It is important to cut out as many of your expenses as you are able for at least a short amount of time. You will find that it is amazing how many things you are able to cut out of your budget without hardly even trying and how little you will really miss those things.

For example, make it a goal to not go out to eat for a whole month. You may not like cooking that much, but by the end of the month you could save at least a few hundred dollars and you will be able to pay down more stuff than ever.

Cut Ties with Credit Cards

A basic rule of thumb, if you have to take out the plastic to make a purchase, you really cannot afford the purchase. Anything that is worth having you can wait for and save up the money until you can afford it straight up. Credit cards come with lots of interest and you will end up paying back way more than it is worth in the long run just paying it off.

Credit cards are sometimes useful though for helping to build up your credits and many people have them in order to help build up some points for a free vacation or for free airline miles.

It can be fine to have a credit card, but you need to make sure that you are only putting what you can pay off each month on it so that the balance goes back to $0. This helps to keep the interest down quite a bit and ensures that you are still getting some of the points that you are looking for to save money elsewhere.

With that being said, if you can't keep your expenses on the credit card down and you tend to overspend on them, it is time to cut them altogether.

If this is one of the places where you have a lot of debt right now, cut up the credit cards and refuse to use them at all. They contain a really high interest rate and should really be the first things that you pay off if possible because they are wasting you a lot of money.

Each person is going to handle their credits cards differently. Some people are able to have these credit cards and pay off the debt on time each month; they keep the credit cards just to get the extra points, miles, or other incentives that come with the card.

On the other hand, there are some people who see a credit card and they are not able to control themselves. They will just keep spending until they hit their limit, and then repeat the process each time that they pay it off.

If you fit into the second group, it is probably not a good idea to have a credit card. Credit cards can be amazing for helping you to build up your credit, but if you max them out and aren't careful about them, they are going to ruin your credit score and aren't worth the time.

It is basically up to the type of person you are. If you are responsible and know that you can pay the credit card off in no time, then go ahead and keep one around for emergencies. But if you are someone who will just spend on it and not be responsible, it is best to find other ways to pay for the things that you want. If you fit into this second group and you already have a credit card, it is time to cut it up and start fresh.

Start Retirement

This is a way to put your money back so that you are not able to spend it while still making sure that you have a safety net for the future. You can use a company plan, especially if your work is willing to match you, or start out your own. This money can be deducted from your paycheck and then you are sure to have some savings.

It is always a good idea to start saving for retirement as early as possible. With the cost of living growing each year, it is going to take a lot of time to save enough to actually retire when you would like to.

There are several ways that you are able to go about doing it. Most people are going to choose to have money taken out of their paychecks each pay period to help with retirement. This is usually taken out before taxes, so it saves you a bit on the tax bill. Plus, many employers have a matching program so you can earn some extra money towards it as well.

If you work for yourself or your company doesn't offer a retirement plan, it is possible to talk to a financial advisor about some of the options. Putting even $100 a month aside is a great place to start and you can always add in more later once you get some of your bills paid down.

The good news is that you are not only saving for a safe financial future later, you are putting away money that you aren't able to spend frivolously elsewhere.

Be Frugal

You should make sure that you are living below the amount that you make. If you end up spending all of the money that you have each month, there is nothing there when emergencies happen or to have some fun with. When you live on the bare minimum you will always have money when it is needed.

Being frugal can be really hard for a lot of people. It requires them to sacrifice a lot so that they can reach success. This means no more going out to eat most nights of the week and instead choosing to cook your own meals.

It means no more going to parties or purchasing the expensive brands at the store. It means cutting the cable cord, stop going to the expensive coffee shop, only getting the things that you really need, and even getting clothes and things from the local thrift shop instead.

Learning how to control your income and some of the things that you are spending your money on can be one of the first steps to seeing some success when you want to get out of debt.

It is impossible to cut out all of the debt if you are spending your money on things that you don't really need or if you are always spending a lot on a credit card that has a huge interest rate. Learning how to monitor and control some of these issues can really make a big difference on how well you are able to become debt free.

Chapter 7: How to Avoid Some of the Most Common Money Traps

There are many money traps that people will fall in to. They have all of the best intentions of saving money and getting their finances all in place, but then they turn around and the money is still all gone. Here are some of the common money traps that you should work to avoid in order to save as much money as possible.

Gym Membership

Many people will be lured in with a great gym membership that is going to allow them to go as much as they want. Despite your best intentions, how likely is it that you will go three or four times a week to the gym?

If you are like most people, you will barely make it four times each month, making that expensive gym membership a lot more expensive. You should take the time to see how much you will actually go and see if there are less expensive gym prices. Or you could purchase a workout video from home and save even more while still getting in some of that good working out that you need to keep the mood up and stay motivated to keep to a budget.

Data Charges

Data on your phone can add up fast, and if you go over your limit, you will be paying high amounts

of it. Any time that you get online or look at your social media sites, it is eating up the data and soon it will all be gone. One way to save on this is to pick a new data plan that allows you to have a bit more each month. You might have to pay more upfront, but you will be saving more when you do not pay on overages.

An even better idea to is to get rid of the data charges all together. There are still some really great phones that rely on just phone calls and texting and they don't have a data charge at all. This can save you hundreds a year and you really won't miss it once you get used to not having this kind of phone around. These plans can be as low at $80 a month or lower while some of the data plans can be well over $100 a month. It may seem like a small savings, but when you add this up over a few years and you avoid some of the extra data charges, you can really save a lot of money over time.

Special Coffee

If you are like many others, you will head out in the morning to get your coffee from Starbucks or another similar store. For a simple cup you could be paying more than $2. If you do this process every day you are spending more than $700 each year and that is just for one cup each day. You can save a lot of money by purchasing a coffee maker, some instant coffee, and a few creamers and making it at home each day. You will also save on the gas that you are using.

This can be true of any of the special drinks or meals that you like to eat. Making your own at home can save you a lot of money in the long run. Stop going out to get breakfast or grabbing something at a local bake shop or deli to eat and make it at home to save a lot of money each day.

Yes, it is going to take some more time from you, but the amount of money will really help to pay down your debts.

Sales

Everyone likes a sale. They feel that it helps them to save money and that they are getting a good deal. The thing is, it is not a good deal if you do not need the product at all. This is just money that you are spending that is unnecessary and you are not saving on anything if the item is not needed. Be careful of flashy emails as well; these are sent out at a certain time so that you have plenty of time to read them and are more likely to spend higher amounts.

Sales are not all that bad all of the time and sometimes they can save you some money, such as when some produce at the store is on sale or your favorite meals are on sale. But if they drive you to make purchases of things that you don't need or you weren't going to spend the money on in the first place, they are harming your budget. Only go for the sale if it is something that you were going to purchase anyway.

Home Fixes

While there is nothing wrong with sprucing up your home to make it better, many people spend a huge part of their budget on things that are not really going to invest in their home. Sticking to a budget on your home can make all of the difference. There are often a lot of little things that you are able to do around the house that will help to spruce it up a bit without costing you as much money.

In addition, if you are doing some of these fixes, you are able to save a lot of money if you are able to do them on your own, rather than hiring a contractor or a professional to do them. These people are going to charge extra money for their time and work on top of the cost of the supplies, and many times you are able to just do it on your own and save a couple hundred dollars or more on getting the work done.

There is nothing wrong with fixing up your home and making it look nice, but you should be careful about how you do this. If you are taking out large loans or spending money that you don't have, you are not working to get your budget in line. Save up for the things that you want and be sure to only do the home fixes that you can afford. Doing some of the work on your own can actually save quite a bit of money so bring out some

YouTube videos and use those to your advantage as well.

Cable

If you are still relying on cable to provide you with entertainment, it is time to cut the cord. Most cable providers are costing you $100 or more a month depending on the package that you have. What would you be able to do with an extra $1200 or more a year to help pay down your debts. Some packages can be even more expensive when you add in some of the fees, and how much television are you really watching.

Most families will find that cable is not really that important to them, they are just used to having it or they are worried about missing out on just a few shows.

When you are budgeting and trying to pay down those debts, you will need to sacrifice a little bit, and this means it s time to cut the cord. Choose to rent movies from the local library or borrow from friends if you really want to save money, or some of the streaming services like Netflix and Hulu are great for watching shows and moves and they cost about $10 a month. It still is a bill to pay, but instead of paying $1200 a year, you are paying $120 a year.

Eating Out

Most Americans spend a lot of money eating out a few times a week. They may be busy trying to get to appointments and athletic events, they want to treat themselves a bit, or they just don't feel like cooking. But if you have a family, you could easily spend over $30 each time that you go out to eat if not more.

If you do this just two times a week, that is going to equate to about $240 a month or $2880 a year! That can quickly add up. Add in that often you will go out and watch a movie or do some other activity on top of it, and you are wasting a good deal of money in the process.

Eating out s supposed to be a treat, not something that you do all of the time. If possible, you should limit the amount of times that you are eating out to just a few times a year. At most you could still save almost $1500 if you cut down from two times a week to just one and that is a good place to start. The more you are able to cut out the eating out and just go with making your own food at home, the more money you are able to save overall.

Expensive Clothes

Many people feel that they need to go out and purchase some of the best brands of clothing in order to fit in or that they need to have something new for every season that they live through. But is it really necessary to spend hundreds of dollars every month or so on clothes that you may not wear all that often? If you are looking at your budget and notice that you spend quite a bit of money on clothing, it is time to make some changes to this.

The first step is to go through your closet and see what is there before you even head out the door to a new store. You may be surprised at how many things are in the back of your closet or dresser that you are able to wear again and you forget all about. Perhaps they will be a few seasons old so people won't remember it at all. Plus, there is nothing wrong with wearing the same outfit over again if it is comfortable and looks nice on you.

If you do happen to need to get something new, which does happen on occasion, make sure to go to a local thrift store. You can find clothes that cost $100 for just a few dollars, helping you to get a whole wardrobe change for the cost of a pair of jeans at your favorite store. Always check here to save a little bit of money.

You would be surprised at how much stuff you are able to get at the local thrift store, and some of it may be brand new. Look around and you may even be able to find some designer outfits and items that are for quite a bit lower compared to purchasing them at a high end store.

Name brands

Some people swear that they are only able to purchase name brands when it comes to the foods they eat, the clothes they wear, and so much more. But name brands are really expensive and usually the generic is just as good; you are simply paying for that fancy name that is on the box or on the label.

The next time that you go to the store, make sure that you only purchase the generic brand of everything that you purchase. Then compare this to an old receipt and see how much you were able to save on the same products.

You will be amazed at how what looks like a little bit on each individual item can add up to quite a bit when you are purchasing a lot of groceries. And when you taste them, it is unlikely that you will notice much of a difference at all so why not try to cut out on the name brand and save that money.

Using Self-Sufficiency to Save Money

When you do not have to waste a lot of money calling someone else in to help you out and giving them some of your hard earned money, it is a great thing. While you may not be able to do everything on your own, no one is able to fix the plumbing, heating, and gas all of the time, doing a few things around the home can save you a bunch of money.

Many of us will waste a lot of money asking someone else to come help us get the work done. While this may be easier, we are able to do quite a bit of this ourselves, especially with the help of YouTube videos, so why not save some of the money and get to work?

Before you give someone a call to come out and help you, take a look at the problem. You may be able to figure out a good solution and save some time and money. Perhaps a little knob got turned around the wrong way and you are able to fix it yourself.

This could save you from calling someone in. Or if something gets stuck in the toilet, trying to get it out yourself is much better than spending $100 or more to get a plumber out. While you may not be able to save money on everything that you do, you can sure save on quite a bit and this can make it worth your time.

The areas where you will really be able to save some money on things is when you start to do it all on your own and make things. For example, instead of hiring someone to mow and water your yard, do it yourself or have one of the kids do it. Instead of having someone come around and put up a new fence with expensive wood, consider going down to a junkyard to see if any boards are left there and if you are able to do it on your own.

Even learning how to sew on your own is a big money saver. Clothes are expensive, even if you are purchasing them second hand at a garage sale or a store. You can always look into make some of your own and see how great you look while saving a ton of money.

A garden is another great way to save some money when it comes to groceries. You can grow almost anything that you would like in a garden and nothing tastes better than growing your own fruits and vegetables rather than relying on the

local store to carry the things that
you would like. Start out small so
that you can get used to the process
and then over time you will be able to
take on more and have a huge garden
in the process.

These are just a few of the ways that
you will be able to save a lot of money
rather than handing over the little bit
extra that you are saving in your
budget to someone else to do the
work for you.

Sure it might be a little more
convenient for someone else to help
you out, but it is going to cost you a
lot in the long run. Try a few of these

out, plus any that you can think of, and start saving the money today.

There are a lot of common money traps that are cutting into your budget and making it hard to stay afloat when you are spending all of this extra money. Learn how to cut some of these out and you will have plenty of extra to help you to get those debts paid off in full.

Chapter 8: How to Invest Your Money the Smart Way

Many times people will earn a paycheck and then just put it towards bills or other things that they want to do for fun. But they are missing out on a great way to ensure that they will earn more money in the long run and be able to pay off some of their bills a bit faster.

Investing your money is basically a way that you are able to take your money and earn more over time. Whether you place it into a savings account or you find a good investment account to work with, you will be able to earn a bit on some of your savings and in some cases, earn another income in a safe and effective manner.

One way that you can make sure that your money is working for you and doing the things that you

would like it to do is to invest. This helps your money to grow with very little effort on your part. The amount you make is going to depend on the risk that you are willing to take; the bigger the risk the more that you could potentially make though you could also lose out as well. Here are some tips for investing your money smartly to make it grow for you.

Savings Account

The first place you should invest is in a savings account. There are often several high interest options available from your bank which allows you to make interest on the money that is inside the account.

Some of these will have minimum amounts that you have to keep in the account so you should watch out for this. These are a great way to make sure that you have some money put away for when you need it and to make money from the interest at the same time.

If you are going to be working with a savings account, make sure that you find one that is higher interest. Most savings accounts are going to be low interest and while it is better than nothing, you are able to find some that have higher interest rates to help you earn more. Keep in mind that you will need to meet some requirements to see the results. For example, most of the higher interest savings accounts will require you to keep a certain amount of money in the account at all times, only do so many transactions a month, or some other requirement.

Retirement Plan

Saving up for your future is an important investment that everyone should take the time to use. This is money that can be taken out of your paycheck and will often grow over time as well so that you are not only saving that money, but you are saving on taxes paid as well. If your employer has a 401k plan available and will match your contribution, make sure to take advantage of it because this is free money.

If this is not available, there are many options for individual retirement plans. Either way, get started on your retirement plan when you are young. This will allow you to have a safe nest when you get to retiring age and you will not have to scramble around in order to get it all done later in life.

Too many people are not putting the money that they should into their retirement plan. Then when they get to their 40s and 50s, they find that they don't have near enough to retire at an early age and they have to keep putting more money towards it for a longer time. As part of your budget, you should consider putting some money inside of a retirement plan.

These traditionally make a good amount of interest over time and this compounds each year to really help you out. Even if you are only able to put a little bit of money into the account each year, it is better than nothing and can really help you out with not being so far behind later on.

Make sure that you explore some of the different options that are available with your retirement plan. For the most part, there are two options. You can pick from the traditional IRA and the Roth IRA Most people who get a retirement plan from their work will be with the traditional IRA. With this option, you will put in some money each month and then it is tax free for that year. In many cases, your employer will choose to contribute a certain percent as well to help you out.

You will be taxed on this money when you retire, usually at a higher rate than today, but since you are getting free money from your employer to help with your retirement, you will find that this is a great and effective method of getting your retirement started.

Another option that you can choose is to work with a Roth IRA. With this option, you will be able to put in money, but you will still have to pay taxes on it right now. Then when you do retire, you will be able to take out money tax free. This can be cost effective because you never know how much taxes are going to change by the time you retire, so it will usually save you some money.

Both of these options can be great for you to choose because you are saving for your retirement. Pick the one that works the best for your situation and make sure that you contribute as much as you can to the retirement plan so that you can retire and be comfortable.

Both of these plans can be really nice, but you need to get one started as soon as possible. With bills, kids, school, and other obligations, it is easy to get distracted and put off your retirement. But starting in your 20s is a much better investment option than waiting until your 30s or 40s. By then it is getting later and you will need to throw quite a bit more money at the account compared to before, just to reach your goals. Even if you are only able to put a small amount towards your retirement, it is better than nothing in those early years.

Finding a good investment

After you have saved a bit of money back, you may want to consider investing some of it. This allows you to make some more, sometimes a full income if you do it properly, and that helps you to pay off bills faster and even save for retirement. In addition to working on a retirement plan as your investment, there are a few other types of investments that you can choose.

Some people like to keep their money safe and they will use bonds. These are basically loans that you will give to a company or a government entity so they can work on a project. They will hold onto the money for a few years, or another predetermined amount of time, and then when that time is up, you will get that money plus some interest back. You will not get as much back as some of the other options, but it is a fairly safe option so you are more likely to get the money back rather than losing it all.

Working in the stock market is another option that a lot of people will work with. There are a lot of options available for those who want to get to the stock market.

You can do a long term investment, penny stocks, day trading, or another option. Most of these can be successful as long as you come up with a good strategy and stick with it. If you are doing some of the riskier options, there is a chance of losing some money, but you can learn pretty quickly and you will start making some great profits.

Another option that works well for some people is real estate investing. With this investment, there are quite a few great options. Some people like to work with rental properties where they are able to earn a profit each month from the rental price of their tenants. Others will flip homes and make a larger profit if they are able to flip the home quickly. Some people find deals on homes and then sell the contracts without actually owning the home. There are many options that come with real estate and figuring out the one that works the best for you is the first step to getting started.

There are many different investment options that you are able to work with. You just need to do a bit of research with them and learn which one is going to work the best for your needs.

Financial Advisor

There are other methods of investing that you can check out, but it is a good idea to get some advice and help before you choose to do this. Talking to a financial advisor is a great idea because it allows you to see the options, get some expert opinions, and get the help that you would need to be successful.

They can talk about options such as stocks, bonds, and so much else. You will then be able to understand the risks and issues that are present with each option so you can make the investment option that is right for you.

Investing is often one of the last thigs that you are going to think about when creating a budget, but it is a great way to help you earn a little bit of extra money on the income that you aren't using and it ensures that you are set up for your future. Make sure to pick at least one of these investments and you are sure to earn a little bit extra and be able to pay off some of those debts a little bit faster.

Chapter 9: Easy Ways to Pay Off Your Debt

Debt is a thing that most Americans are familiar with. It is something that can hold you back from reaching the potential that you want, something that makes it almost impossible to get some of the things that you need. Debt can come from a lot of different places such as credit cards, student loans, mortgage, loans, and other things. Here are some of the steps that you can take in order to tackle the debt that you have in no time at all.

Assemble the debt

Before you are able to pay it all off, you need to know how much you have. Bring out all of the statements you have for your mortgage, credit cards, student loans, and everything else. This is going to force you to look at the number that you have and see just how much it all is. This can help you to get a realistic picture of the way that things are in your life and you can then work to cut it down.

There are many tools that you are able to use to help you get a handle on your debt. But having it in one place can help you to know how much you owe and how much you need to tackle. You can set up goals for kicking out that debt, get a graph that helps you to see how far you have come and so far you have to go before being done.

Look at your budget

This is going to help you to determine if you have a little bit of extra money that can be put towards the debt each month. The more that you can pay on these debts, even if it is a small amount, the better off you will be because it saves a lot of interest.

We spent some time in this guidebook talking about the different ways that you can set up a budget. But you really need to take the time to look through the budget and find where you can make cuts.

There are always places where you can make some adjustments, add in more money, cut out some things, and make changes. Always set it up so that you review your budget a few times a year to make sure that you are on the right track and that you aren't falling off or spending more again than you should.

Make extra payments

Any time that you have the money to do this, making an extra payment can make a huge difference. Just $50 a month on a credit card payment or other loan can end up saving you thousands of dollars due to less interest accumulating. This might seem like such a little thing, but when you are done you will be amazed at how much you are saving.

There are several ways that you are able to do this. Some people choose to do the snowball effect. With this, you will take the debt that is the largest, or the one with the highest interest rate, and then put the extra money that you have towards that one each month. Then when that one is all paid off, whether that is over a few months or a few years, you will take that extra payment, as well as the full payment from that big loan, and put it towards the second highest loan. And then you keep up on this, adding more and more payments to the debts until they are paid off.

It is always best to go with the loan that has the highest interest or the biggest payment each month and get that paid down, but you can honestly pick any of the debts that you have. Some like to start with the smallest amount because it can give them some motivation to get the work done when they see some of those smaller debts getting paid off, rather than waiting around for the bigger ones to get done. You can do it either way, just make sure to take the one payment and move it over to the next debt when you are done with it.

The first debt or two will take the longest to pay off, but by the time you are to the last few, you are going to have quite a few payments going towards it. If you pay off three debts that were $200 each, that means the fourth one is going to have an extra $600 a month going to it, and that can pay it off in no time.

The important thing to remember here is that while you are paying off the debts, you will need to pay the minimum on all of the debts each month so that you don't get the extra fees and other costs on the account. Then if you have any extra to spend, you can throw it at the debts to pay off faster, but always pay at least the minimum each month.

Find ways to save

There is usually going to be some method that you can find that will save you some money each month. Instead of watching the expensive cable package, get a smaller one or get rid of cable altogether and go outside or watch movies. Get rid of the smartphone and get a basic plan on a basic phone or switch carriers. Turn off lights in your home to save on electricity. Purchase your clothes at a thrift store rather than the mall. Find coupons or consider going with the generic brand.

These are just a few places where you would be able to save some money and can put it towards your loans and debt.

One trick that works well for a lot of people is to pay themselves first.

Before you go out and pay for your bills or worry about paying of those debts a bit more, you should put a little bit of money back into savings each month. If you decide on a certain amount, even if it is just $100 a month, you should take that out of your account and put it into your own savings account before you pay for anything else.

Over time, this is going to cause you to have a lot of extra savings and you won't have to worry about doing it the other way around. Most people don't save because they pay off everything first and they end up not having enough leftover, but doing the saving first can help you to get it done and then you can worry about the other bills later with what is leftover.

Extra income

In some cases, you might be able to bring in a little extra income that could help with the debt. Taking on a second job or at least more hours at your current job can give you some more money to play with. Try selling some of the things that you own and do not use any longer to get some money. Freelance work that goes with your skills can also help as well. This is money that you should put towards paying off your extra bills and then into savings.

There are many ways that you are able to earn an extra income and not all of them are going to require you to go out and get a second job. If your current job and your schedule have some room, you can go and get a second job. This can be a great way to earn some extra money in your free time and when there is a little bit of extra money available, you are more likely to pay off your debts and put some money into savings. Even if you just do it for a little bit to pay down a debt or two, it can make a big difference in your budget and your financial future.

For some people, it may be difficult to go through and get a second job that works around your current schedule. There are still other options that you are able to go with. Some people choose to take on some freelance work to help earn a bit of extra cash at least while they are paying down the bills.

This can include doing some writing, answering surveys, or doing some random chores around town to help people out around town. Any amount of money that you earn through this method should be placed towards your debts or your savings to help you get things taken care of.

Learning how to earn some extra money or get those debts paid down quickly. And the faster that you are able to pay off some of those debts, the easier it is to use that money to save for retirement or to have some extra money that is for something fun. While you may have to live uncomfortably tight for a bit or get another side job, paying off your debts can be a rewarding experience that you will enjoy.

Chapter 10: How to Make More Money to Pay Off Debts Faster

If you are looking to make your budget more manageable or pay off some of the debts that you owe, you might want to look into make more money. While it is possible to ask your boss for a raise, this does not always work and you might still not make enough to get ends to meet. There are many ways that you can make some money on the side that can help with your budget. Some of the methods that you can try include:

Getting a second job

Sometimes you can fill in at different jobs on the weekends or at nights.

This would be a steady income that would be able to boost your budget. You will need to look for something that is going to fit in with your current schedule to make this work, but taking on a few extra hours in your free time is a great way to add more money to your budget and to ensure that you are able to pay off the debts.

While many people are able to just rearrange their budget a little bit and they are fine with getting things paid off with some hard work, there are others who may just have too much debt and not enough income. Adding in at least a few hours a week, or perhaps both you and your spouse get an extra job, and you are able to pay off things faster than ever.

Remember with this one that if the second job is starting to interfere with your regular job, you will need to stop. You don't want to lose your main form of income in order to take care of the second job, or you are in a worse state than before. Strive to find a second job that works with the first job, and then you will start to appreciate some of those extra funds that are there when you need them the most.

Focus groups

Various companies are looking to get opinions on their products and services and in some cases they will pay for it. Often these will only take a few hours at most of your time and you can make some great money. This can provide some great information to the companies that are paying you, and it only takes a few hours of your time on occasion. In addition, doing some paid clinical studies can pay thousands of dollars and you simply need to follow the rules and sometimes stay overnight a few times to get the money.

Surveys

This is like the focus group, but often the pay, as well as the time commitment, will be less. You can fit these in during your free time and enjoy having a little bit extra at the end of the month. Keep in mind that these can sometimes take a lot of time to do and they don't pay the most. But if you are looking for something simple to do when you need to waste some time, surveys can be the best option for you.

Rolling billboards

Depending on the area you live in and how much driving you do, you might be able to get paid for putting a billboard on your vehicle. A company will pay you to put a simple applique on your car and then do your normal driving. This allows them to get some advertising while you make money driving around.

Why not make a little bit of extra money each month by putting a few advertisements on your car? You will still just drive around to the locations where you need to, such as work and the grocery store, and the company you are advertising for will get some extra marketing.

Sell your stuff

It is time to do some cleaning around the house. You will find a lot of things that you no longer need and you can then get rid of it for some profit. Do a garage sale or sell your stuff online to make some extra money. Most of us have some extra stuff that is hanging around the house and just taking up space. This may not be a permanent thing that you can do to make money of the long term, but selling some of the items around your home, rather than throwing it all away, can help you to make some money that can go to paying off a debt a little bit more.

Freelance work

Depending on the kinds of skills you have, you might be able to do some freelance work. There are many companies that will hire you to do a few projects for them. They will hire you to get this work done and you can make a good paycheck while saving the company some money as well. There is a lot of freelance work that you are able to do and when you break it down per hour, you will find that it is easier to make a good income than your regular job.

There are a lot of different types of freelance work that you are able to do. You can choose to write some of your own eBooks or write for other companies. It is possible to do graphic design, advertising, logo design, computer work, and so much more. Find what your specialty is and then go out there and look for some of the work that you need to make it a result.

Chapter 11: Simple Ways to Cut Down on the Bills

So far we have spent some time talking about a few simple things that you can do to get your budget in line and to make sure that you have a little extra money coming in to help you out. But another option that you can do that really helps out is to cut down on your bills.

There are only so many ways that you are able to bring more money into your budget. You can only work so many hours, do so many projects, and sell so much stuff. If you don't figure out how to cut down on some of the bills, it won't matter how much you work, you will still have a lot of debts to deal with. So the next step is to learn some simple things that you can do in order to cut down on those bills and to stretch your income just a bit further.

While there are many ways to bring in more money to your budget, you will only have so much time available in your day and you might not be able to take on the extra responsibilities. Instead, you might have to determine some ways to cut down on the bills that you already have. When you cut down on the bills, you can save a lot of money that can be used in other parts of your life.

Pack Lunch

One area that people will spend a lot of money is on lunch. They will go to a local place by their work or go to the cafeteria and spend their hard earned money to get something to eat. When you make your own lunch each day, you are able to save money as well as eat something that is much healthier for your body.

This can also be said of eating out. When you make meals at home, especially freezer meals that are ready when you are, you are going to end up saving a ton of money in the long run. The fewer times that you eat out, the more money that will be in your budget to use on other things.

Make coffee at home

Instead of going out and getting coffee a few times a day, make some of your own at home. This could save you hundreds of dollars each year and it is much cheaper to purchase your own coffee maker and coffee mix. If you are someone who feels that they need a cup of coffee each day, make sure that you make some at your home rather than going to the Starbucks or another location to get it.

For example, let's say that you get a coffee for $3 each day at Starbucks. By the end of the month, you have spent $90 or more on coffee, which ends up being $1095. That small cup of coffee that didn't seem like such a big deal is costing you more than $1000 a year to maintain. You could choose to go with making your own coffee at home, which ends up costing just pennies a day, or give up your coffee or specialty drink, and see what a difference it makes on your budget.

This can apply to many different things in your life. If you have a specialty drink, go out to eat, or do something else that seems like a small expense, add up how much you spend on it each year, and then you may be more willing to cut it out of your budget.

Throw out cable

Cable is a large bill that many people have to deal with each month. Often they will be spending over $100 a month on this service and other than a few channels, it is going to waste. Cut out the cable bill and go for an online streaming service or rent movies. There are also some local channels that you can get for free so you can still watch some of your favorite shows without paying anything.

There are many other ways to get the entertainment that you are looking for from cable. Many people will choose to get Hulu or Netflix to help keep them entertained. These often cost about $10 a month, while cable can cost $100 or more a month. That is a huge savings over a year if you are able to live with some of the offerings on these streaming services and even if you decide to go with both, you are saving money.

Other activities that you can do rather than watching television, if you would like to save even more money, includes going on a walk, reading a book (which you can get for free at your local library), visiting with friends, doing a puzzle, doing some surveys or making some extra money, and so much else. Cable is a big expense that a lot of people have yet to get rid of, but it is often way more expensive than other options and it is best to get it cut out.

Utilities

Utilities are able to creep way up on you each month and can cost a bundle. You should make sure to turn off the lights whenever you are not using them to save some money. Only use the water when you need it and try to cook a few meals at a time to save on heating up the oven for supper. Keep the heat low in the winter and the air conditioner down during the summer. Bundles or hanging out outside can help to save on these which will really save on your budget.

Go down to one vehicle

Some families will have two or three vehicles that they are driving around all the time. There are several problems with this on your budget. First, you are most likely paying off two different car payments, which could be more than $200 a month in payments for each of them.

Then you are paying to license and register these each year, which will add another bill that you have to deal with. Insurance can cost quite a bit as well and you have to pay this for each vehicle. If you have to pay of the maintenance, the parking spots, and more, this can add up to quite a bit each month.

Going down to one car can make a big difference with this. With going down to one car, you can save on insurance, gas, parking, registration, and a car payment, which could end up saving you thousands a year. If you are able to get by with just one vehicle, sell the car and use that money to pay off other debts.

Gas

Driving to each place you need to go can eat up your budget. Try walking to some of the places or plan out a route that is going to be the most efficient to save on the gas bill. Also, plan out the trips so that you are only having to go to the store once a week instead of going several times.

It is really hard to budget for the price of gas considering that keeps going up and down. So limiting the amount of times that you drive can make a big difference. Try to go to just one store and make out a list before you go so that you are not missing out on things that you need. Walk to the library or to the park and get in some good exercise rather than having to drive there. The less you have to spend on gas each month, the more money that goes into your pocket.

Groceries

Your family has to eat each month, but this does not mean that you cannot save some money on the groceries that you are eating. Try taking the time to use coupons to lower the bill or you can even go with the generic brands. You get the same great tasting food without the high cost.

There are actually quite a few ways that you will be able to save on groceries. The first one is to look through some of the ads in your area. You may find that there are widely different prices on the items that you like to purchase the most and you can get them for a bit less. Some stores will price match so you can just go to one store and get it all, and then just show the coupon to the cashier to get the discount. Other times you will have to visit a few stores so make sure that the price of gas is going to be worth the savings.

If you have a smartphone, you can scan your receipts and earn some money back. Some companies will offer you money back and this can save you a lot of money in the long run. They use this information to see some of the buying habits of their typical user, so keep those receipts and scan them in.

Purchasing items when they are in season can save money. During the winter, there maybe some kinds of fruits available, but if they are considered out of season, their price is going to be way higher. Pick in season fruits and vegetables, as well as other items, and you can save a lot of money in the process.

Eating out can really cut into your family budget so make sure that you eat in as much as possible. Many American families end up eating out three or more times a week, and this can add up. For those few meals, you could end up paying over $100 for that convenience, and think of all the groceries that you would be able to purchase with that money instead. Why not consider making more meals at home and eating out less to save money and help you to lose weight.

Learning how to reduce the amount that you are paying on things each month can make a big difference. While it does help to bring in more money to your budget if possible, there is only so much that you are able to make and so many hours that you can work. If you learn how to cut out some of your expenses, in addition to raising your income a bit, you will find that there is quite a bit of money left over to play with each month.

Chapter 12: How to Reduce
Your Taxes to Save More Money

One way that you are able to save more money and make more out of the income that you have is to learn how to reduce your taxes. This is money that is given to the government and that you will have to lose out of your income that is not working for you.

Tax season is one of the best times for those who are working on a budget, as long as you make plans properly. You will need to sort through some of your finances and learn how they are able to help you during tax time. For example, you could put some money into a retirement plan and the have less money to tax during tax season, you could use some of your student loan interest payments to increase your tax return, or have more withheld out of your check to help lessen the tax burden.

Depending on how much planning you do ahead of time, you may find that you are able to get a good return when tax season comes around. The best thing that you can do with this is to put it towards one of your debts, rather than spending it on a vacation or something else frivolous. Think of what an extra few hundred dollars could do to get that loan paid off a little bit faster and you didn't have to work harder to make it happen.

After a few years of getting a little bit extra back at the end of the year, you can quickly get some of those debts paid down and you can then use that money to help with your retirement, to put some in savings, or to have a bit of fun. But make sure that you are using the money responsibly and use these tips to help you to at least reduce your tax bill, or to get a refund, when tax season shows up.

Here are three ways that you will be able to reduce the amount that you are paying in taxes.

Reduce income that is taxable

The government is going to start out with taxing your whole income. You need to find some ways that you will be able to reduce the amount that they will be taxing. This is going to make more money in your pocket. First off, you will be getting more of that money, even though it is in your paycheck still. In addition, you will be taxed in a lower tax bracket which can save you some money as well.

One of the best ways to reduce the amount of income that you are taxed on is to put money into your retirement accounts. There are various ones available and you can choose the ones that are the best for your needs. This will save you money now plus helps to ensure that you have something to fall back on when you retire.

Increase Deductions

Another way that you can reduce the amount of taxes that you are paying is to find more deductions that you can add in. Deductions are what you can use in order to reduce the amount of income you make so that it not as much is taxed. Some things that you might be able to deduct would be charitable donations, fees for registering your car, fees that you paid for getting the taxes done, and even some of the things that you had to buy for your job. You will have to make sure that you keep receipts and check that you are deducting the right things, but if you do it right, you can end up saving more on your taxes and could even get more money back to use in savings or other methods.

Tax deductions are a great way to make sure that you are reducing the amount of tax that you are paying so that you can keep more of that money in your pocket. Even if you don't end up getting a tax return with them, at least you will be able to reduce the amount that you have to pay in at the end of the year. Talk to your tax advisor and find out what some of the best tax deductions for your situation will be.

Look at tax credits

In addition to the deductions, you will be able to take advantage of some of the tax credits that are available. While they will not reduce the amount of money that can be deducted from your taxes, they can give you some free money from the government. Some examples of tax credits that you can qualify for include energy saving tax credit, education credits, child and dependent care expenses, child tax credit, and earned income tax credit. When you are doing your taxes, make sure to check out if you qualify for these credits to see if you would be able to save more money.

There are many different tax credits that you are able to find when you are working on your tax return. You can get credits for kids in your family, for being married, for adding clean energy to your home, and so much more. If you are uncertain about the amount or type of tax credits that you are able to get, you should meet with a tax professional. They will be able to help you to get the most out of your tax return each year while making sure that you don't miss out on anything.

Remember that if you do happen to get a refund from your taxes that you should put it towards something that can help you to get ahead with your debts. It is tempting to put it towards vacations or other purchases, but if you are serious about paying off the debt, you need to make sure that you are putting that money to good use.

Chapter 13: The Importance of Starting a Savings Account for Your Financial Health

As mentioned a bit above, it is important that you learn how to save. Most people simply do not know how to save. They may know the basics, but they will just spend all of their money and say that they will start saving later on or when they make more money.

The problem is that if you are not able to save early on you are going to have more issues with saving as time goes on. It is important to start saving today, even if it is just a few dollars each week. Anything is going to help in the long run and it is better to have this extra money on hand in case you need it later on.

One of the best pieces of advice that you can use to help you get ahead is to pay yourself first. Rather than paying off all of your bills and then hoping there is some left for savings at the end of the month, you will pay yourself first.

Often we assume that we will get to saving later on, but then things come up, we eat out a few extra times, or something else and then nothing is left at the end of the month.

Instead of doing this, you need to put aside some money for savings each month. Then the rest of it can be used for bills or that extra stuff that you want to do. But if you put the money into savings right from the beginning, it is easier to stay on track and ensures that the money isn't gone by the end of the month.

Even if you are only able to put away a $50 a month, it is better than nothing, but do it right at the beginning of the month to ensure that you don't spend it all before you get to your savings goal.

It is important to save because it is not always easy to predict what is going to happen in the future. You may have an accident, lose your job, or need to get something fixed on the car. Without savings, you are either stuck or you are going to have to use your credit card and hope you can pay it off without all of the extra in interest hurting the bank. In addition, it is always better to save up for some of the things that you want because it makes them more valuable to you and prevents the extra money and debt that comes with interest rates.

There are many different reasons why you may want to consider having a savings ready on hand to help you out. Some of these include

- A cushion for emergencies—
  emergencies are going to
  happen all of the time and you
  may not be able to do much
  about it. Many things, such as
  a medical expense because of
  an accident, needing to put a
  new roof on the car, losing
  your job, having the car break
  down, or something else are
  not things that you plan on,
  but they are still going to cost
  you a lot of money and they
  need to be taken care of.
  Without savings, you will still
  have to pay for them, and
  usually it will be over a longer
  period of time with interest

accruing. Usually the fact that you do not have a savings is the reason that you are in debt. If you are able to put back a small amount of money each month while paying off your debts, you are putting yourself in a good situation for never being in debt again.

- Retirement—no matter how much you may say it now, you are not going to work until the day you die. Even if nothing bad happens, like poor health, you are going to get tired of working and will want to spend some time with your grandkids, traveling, and doing things other than working for someone else. Putting together a retirement plan is a great way to start saving and this is money that you will be able to use when you are older. Talk to your financial advisor, or find one, and you can start saving early for this critical part of your life. The earlier you are able to start saving, as well as the bigger amount you can put in, the better off you will be when it comes time to retire. Most people underestimate the amount that they are going to need in order to retire and this can be harmful. You will need a lot of money for a place to live, medical bills, and so much else and with inflation, this money can be eaten up in no time. Having a retirement plan can ensure that you are taken care of as you age.

- Average life expectancy—it is more likely than ever that you are going to live to ripe old age and need to have money to make it through. You are probably still going to retire at the same age as your parents and grandparents, but if you live an extra 10 years, you are going to need more money. Medical bills, inflation, and housing costs are also likely to go up and without a savings in place, you may have to find other means in order to pay all of these things off. Starting your savings now can really make a difference later on.

- Education—the cost of education has quickly been on the rise. It is costing more than ever in order to get an education. Some of the debt that you may be dealing with is due to the fact that you are paying off your education. But what happens if you need to go back to school sometime in the future? Do you really want to go through the whole ordeal of paying off student loans again and dealing with the interest? Having some savings put back for your educational expenses can really help you out as well. Some people will also choose to help their children out through college. It is important to note that you do not have to do this and if it is going to harm your own savings and put you back in debt, do not do it. Your children can work for the education or take out their own loans but your retirement and finances should come first. But if you are in the right financial situation to help, you will find that savings will help

with the huge rise in
educational costs by the time
your child goes to school.

- Pay for the things that you
  want or need—many people
  have become too attached to
  the loans or the use of credit
  cards that make it very easy for
  them to purchase the things
  that they would like to have.
  They like the idea that they can
  get the item right that moment
  rather than waiting weeks or
  even months while they save
  up for it. While it might be an
  ok idea to use your credit card
  in an emergency or in order to
  build up your credit score, you

should use it very little. It is better to save and pay for the item right out rather than putting it on a card and then having to pay much more on the interest. Plus, you are going to value the item much more if you actually had to work for it.

When you do not put some money into savings or into an investment, such as your retirement plan, you are pretty much just asking for a risk to occur to you. It is better to have this money put away in case you ever need it rather than worrying about how you will pay for something when an emergency occurs.

Another tip is that as your income goes up, or you get a bonus at work, don't go and spend that money on going out or lavishly. Put most of that money into savings or into your retirement to ensure that it is used in the proper manner rather than just wasted.

While savings might seem like it is the last thing that you should be worrying about when you have bills to pay, mouths to feed, and a million other places that your money needs to go, any little bit can help. Even if you are only able to put about $50 a month back, it is going to add up over time and you will be really thankful

that you did it when the time comes
down the road. Just put in any
amount that you can and then it will
be there when you need it most.

Chapter 14: Getting Ready for Early Retirement

No one wants to spend the rest of their life working, especially if it is a job that they do not like. They want to be able to retire on time, if not earlier, so that they are able to enjoy life and do the things that they have always dreamed of.

Luckily, there are a few steps that you can take to ensure that you are set up for early retirement. If you are able to start early and make a plan for success, you are going to see some big changes in no time.

Here are some of the things that you should watch out for and do if you would like to retire early.

Look at current finances

To make plans for your future finances, you first need to determine where your current finances are. This gives you a good picture of how much you have, how much you will need to save, and if it is even realistic to retire early. There are a few basic questions that you should ask yourself to figure out if early retirement is the right choice for you. These questions include:

1. What expenses will you have when you retire

2. How much money do you need to cover retirement costs?

3. How much do you need to save in order to get this done?

Determine savings shortfalls

You should then determine the date that you would like to retire and then divide the years that are left to see how much you would like to have saved. For example, if you are planning on retiring in about 20 years and you need to get $500,000 saved in that time, you will need to be able to save $25,000 each year to make it. Depending on how much you are making each year and your current spending, you might find that it is difficult to do this.

Scrub up the budget

Your budget is going to have to be really tight if you would like to retire early. You will need to find ways to make more money and save more money in order to get to that goal and you will need to do it for the long term.

Take a full look at the budget that you have and the budget that you want and find out where you can make some changes. Are you going to need to get a second job for a few years to save a comfortable amount?

Will you need to stop going out to eat every week for that money? You have to take a look and determine what can be done to save for early retirement.

Save as much as you can

While you may not be able to put back the maximum in the beginning, especially if you are trying to pay down some other debts, it is still a good idea to start saving as much as you can. The more that you are able to save, the better your nest egg into retirement is going to look. And as your income goes up, you should put more money into your retirement account, rather than changing your standard of living.

Each year that you are able to put in money to the account you will get a bigger amount in there, and then add in the compound interest you will see a big difference between putting in as little as possible and putting in as much as possible. You may have to scrounge a bit and have some tough years while you are paying off the other debts as well, but you will find that it is much better to suffer a bit when you are younger rather than dealing with this when you are older and ready to retire.

Start early

The earlier you start on your retirement, the better off you will be. If you are able to start off in your 20s, you are able to save thousands more over time, even with contributing less than you would if you started in your 30s or 40s. You have to remember the beauty of compound interest; when your money is in the retirement accounts, you are earning interest on it each year. So the more years that the money is in that account, the more interest you can earn.

Of course, when you are saving for ten extra years or more, not only are you earning more in interest, you are putting more money into the account as well. And this is really going to add up the more years you hold onto that account and put in money. So make sure to start that retirement account now, even if you can only put in a few dollars a month, and you will be able to sit back and enjoy a nice retirement later on.

Be diligent

This is going to be tough, but you need to stick with the plan that you make. There is no way to get to an early retirement if you do not stick with the plan and make sure that you are getting it done properly. While it might be tough on occasion, you need to stay with it. Just think about that nice retirement that you would like and how nice it will be whenever things get difficult.

Make Changes

You might find that the first budget you created is not quite working to get you to the goal that you want. You might have thought at one time that it would work out great, but things came up and you need to make some changes to it. Every few months take a look at the plan and see how it is working and if it is doing the job that you would like it to do.

Many of us are worried about our retirement. We want to be able to go into retirement and enjoy the life that we have after working hard for so many years. Having a good retirement plan in place can help to make this a bit easier. Follow these steps and you are sure to have the retirement that you always dreamed about.

Conclusion

Getting out of debt is a dream that many people have. They are tired of having to pay down care payments and student loans and other debts all of the time, watching their money disappear all of the time. But this is a reality that many people have to face, and it can really drain you.

Sometimes the best way to get out of debt is to make a plan and stick with it. There are many steps that you can take to come up with a budget, figure out how much you have to spend, and get things done. With some of the simple steps that are inside of this guidebook, you will quickly be able to get your finances in order and start paying off some of those debts in no time.

Keep in mind that working on reaching financial freedom is not something that is going to happen overnight. It is something that takes a lot of time and dedication. But if you are able to stick with it, you will find that your debts can get paid off much faster than before, and the amount of money that you are able to save in interest and fees is going to add up quickly.

No matter who you are, it is easy to get started on making your own budget and getting those debts paid off. Take a look through this guidebook and soon you will have your debts paid off and you can use your money for what matters most to you rather than seeing it disappear to your debts each month.

www.ingramcontent.com/pod-product-compliance
Lightning Source LLC
Chambersburg PA
CBHW030634220526
45463CB00004B/1522